PLEXIGLASS

ALSO BY MARGO PERIN

*How I Learned to Cook & Other Writings
on Complex Mother Daughter Relationships*

Only the Dead Can Kill: Stories from Jail

The Opposite of Hollywood

Spiral of Gratitude

PLEXIGLASS

Margo Perin

WHOA
NELLY
PRESS

Copyright © 2020 by Margo Perin

All rights reserved. No part of this publication may be reproduced, distributed, or transmitted in any form or by any means, including photocopying, recording, or other electronic or mechanical methods, without the prior written permission of the publisher, except in the case of brief quotations embodied in critical reviews and certain other noncommercial uses permitted by copyright law. For permission requests, write to the publisher, addressed "Attention: Permissions Coordinator," at the address below.

Whoa Nelly Press
3442 Sacramento Street
San Francisco, CA 94118
www.whoanellypress.com

Publisher's Cataloging-in-Publication data
Perin, Margo, author
Plexiglass: poems / Margo Perin.
ISBN 978-0-578-68117-7
1. Perin, Margo—Poetry. 2. Poetry—Criminal Justice. 3. Poetry—Incarceration.

FIRST EDITION

Some of the stories and poems quoted in this volume were published in *Only the Dead Can Kill: Stories from Jail* (ed. Margo Perin, 2006).

Angela Y. Davis, excerpt from "Introduction—Prison Reform or Prison Abolition?" from *Are Prisons Obsolete?* Copyright ©2003 by Angela Y. Davis. Reprinted with the permission of The Permissions Company, LLC on behalf of Seven Stories Press, www.sevenstories.com.

Photographs courtesy of Chris Stewart and Margo Perin.

The former San Francisco County Jail, featured in image in this volume, was replaced by, and advertised as, *a new structure of glass, steel and concrete ... a gleaming new centerpiece ... with an indoor recreation area—* and, therefore, discontinued access to the natural world.

Book Design by Lili Paredes

For Marci Klane, as always

And for all the women and men, girls and boys
families and friends, communities and neighborhoods
seen and unseen in these pages

AUTHOR'S NOTE

There are more than 2.3 million people incarcerated in the United States, with another 4.7 million on parole or probation. Thousands more are imprisoned in 200 Immigration and Customs Enforcement jails and detention centers. The individuals, families, and communities impacted before, during, and after incarceration comprise many millions more, including 6 million children.

The intention behind this collection of interrelated poems is to shed light on the story within the story within the story of the prison industrial complex, which is fueled by poverty and racism. In the words of Angela Y. Davis in *Are Prisons Obsolete?* (Seven Stories Press, 2003), "The prison … functions ideologically as an abstract site into which undesirables are deposited, relieving us of the responsibility of thinking about the real issues afflicting those communities from which prisoners are drawn in such disproportionate numbers. This is the ideological work that the prison performs—it relieves us of the responsibility of seriously engaging with the problems of our society, especially those produced by racism and, increasingly, global capitalism."

The experiences expressed by men and women in San Francisco County Jail and men incarcerated in San Quentin State Prison during my years of teaching creative writing workshops there mirror the lives of millions of people hidden behind plexiglass, seen and not seen. I hope the voices in this volume speak to you as they did me.

FOREWORD

In these
PAGES or MONUMENT
Margo Perin has placed her eyes, her ears, her mind, and her heart for 12? 20? years (*and counting …*) in the work of facilitating the writing of certain prisoners in certain prisons in the United States. (Please note that by "certain", what I mean to point out is how numerous these buildings—the prisons—are in this country known as the "land of the free.") In her author's note, she records the figure of 6,000,000 incarcerated people, roughly the population of Finland. Later she clarifies to me, a Mexican poet, *It's hard to be precise with this, but more than 2.3 million people are incarcerated in the United States, with another 4.7 million on parole or probation. The individuals, families, and communities impacted before, during, and after incarceration comprise many millions more, including 6 million children.*

This volume of poetry lends a voice to prisoners and their devastating declarations. Moreover, the voices here in this book can be multiplied to mirror the voices of the entire population of incarcerated men and women in the United States.

The prisoners' self-portraits inside this volume are made with very few strokes. They record what is lost and establish what the irreversible structure of a face looks like, due to what has been snatched from these men and women: privacy, nourishment, natural light, air, physical contact with their loved ones; in short, what we know of as "freedom".

What is absorbed in the ink of *Plexiglass* is the rhythm in which they spoke, and the pattern of pain expressed in their writings. They: the prisoners. They who no longer live behind bars or doors, but behind the hard and transparent material known as "plexiglass". Their cell: similar to a cage in a zoo, with not a single moment of privacy, with the human condition related to the private=the intimate also snatched from them.

In the end, many are African descendants of an iniquitous act (stealing person by person from their houses in that continent) and the making of each person a slave. Later "liberated" as a result of the Civil War and quickly restricted from society again, and classified as criminals until the prison population grew from hundreds of thousands to millions, as the author notes (and counting …). To this population we can add Latinxs, Indigenous Americans, Pacific Islanders, and Asian American communities—the point being that to be Black or Brown in the United States of America is treated as a crime.

However, here is a poet, whose nose was "fixed" against her will, who lost a baby against her will, who lost her spleen, a breast, and a series of dwellings overnight, without a farewell. (To know more, read her poignant book, *The Opposite of*

Hollywood, that describes her family moving from one place to another due to their father being a criminal, something the children were unaware of). Therefore, there is a poet who knows loss and criminality, and who has chosen to work with these prisoners for almost a quarter of a century, and is still working, now with young people targeted for prison. And with some of them writing about their own inhuman, superhuman pain and their aberrant memories.

In their orange jumpsuits, they are walked into classrooms lit by fluorescence, given only one pencil, issued only one page. Margo Perin provided the space for them to speak, and much later, when she was no longer working there, what they said had occupied a space in her head, and soaked in the rain that drowned them, became the ink carrying their voices, the voices of *Our society's disappeared*.

Margo Perin starts this book with the line *Who lurks in the shadows of our midnights?* The pages that come after show a refined ear to a field of pain, an ear that names the falling of the axe on the necks of certain races. An ear that listens to the naming of the inhuman and places on center stage their bleeding at the core of injustice. This was Margo Perin's method: to listen. With her literary wellspring: her own cellular cells.

>Three-inch pencils and paper in hand
>(one eraser each)
>They can become the authors
>of their own—cells

Following the general idea of modernism, which is being able to see one thing from many angles at the same time, where, for example, five strokes can replicate the principal gesture of a person, there is something parallel here. These five strokes (phrases written by prisoners) are the five events of a life that show on the face, a gesture facing death, as when a face is deeply contracted in front of a tragic event. That gesture now occupies the place of the face. And with the multiple natural movements of a face when one is free, now gone. Just those five facts, those five events, reduce a life to a gesture.

My stepfather said choose me or him
and she chose him—Janice
I've been homeless since I was twelve
When I refused to do the laundry she burned my books—Peter
That way I learned the importance of education
My babysitter made me stick
my pee-pee in my sister—Tom

It is significant, the speed at which one can describe a destroyed life, either by a person's own volition or by the accumulation of injustice in their country. It is significant that a book of poems manages to capture that fact. Later, as you advance further into the book, you see that she makes another bold move.

She turns the book into a monument.

DEDICATED TO ALL
MEN AND WOMEN LIVING INSIDE

The voice that honors these dispossessed millions, in this case the voice of Margo Perin, who ties their invisibility among the "free", "the alive", "the active", becomes the *raison d'être* of this monument. The descendants of the slaves in the United States are counted here as the disappeared. This book is their monument. And it is a monument.

I write this foreword with particular emotion because this country known as the free world is in the middle of a pandemic (this is June 2020), when a movement has exploded; a movement that occupies their streets, in part due to a *coup de grâce*, the assassination of another Black man, George Floyd, at the hands of the police (by knee to be more precise, asphyxiated by the knee of a policeman, while he, the victim, repeated the phrase, "I can't breathe"). This book has always been necessary, because poetry exists completely outside discourse, it exists in the heavens and it exists outside logic, and it is here to repair the failed part of our logic. And now more than ever in the summer of 2020 and from now on, this book is indispensable. This is a book that should be read by every person to whom these invisibles are unknown. It must be read in schools, in parks, in bed, and in all those spaces that are not occupied by the disappeared, because they are not in schools, or in parks, or in beds.

To emphasize how seldom white people end up in prison, in comparison to people of color, one of the prisoners writes:

If you're white you done something real wrong—Terrance

						black	brown
					black black
			brown brown
						black black
					black black
				white black
				brown brown
		brown black			black
		black			black brown
				brown white
				brown black
		brown			brown black
			black black black
			jail probation prison
				parole prison
				prison prison
		parole jail	probation prison

There will be readers who will find a valley of rhythm in these pages, placed in this book by a woman who lost her nose and gained a third ear.

    And so it goes on from there … this book that takes the best legacy of Edgar Lee Masters and the Decameron. And all those books that do not consider hell a place separate from heaven. Among them:

Staring at life's distortions through **Plexiglass**

Valerie Mejer Caso
Mexico

PLEXIGLASS

Who lurks in the shadows of our midnights?

A draft of old sweat body-soaked
clothes wafts through hallways
The sores and wounds of outrageous
fortune bleeding through air
stifling hot—or cold

Warehouse-sized rooms overflowing with children nobody
wants—or wanted too much
Bodies scarred with the semen and broken dreams of damaged
adult(s) who raised or braised
them encased in concrete and steel ribs
of two- and three-tiered sagging bunks
on which languish decaying bodies
of men and women cementing
the soft shell of two and a half
million children who never were—and counting

Slipping in and out of shadows seeking
matter among perennial strangers and not
on blank pages lined confined and
not—letting names of *this* and *that*

                        emerge into light

Wanting not wanting to be
found men and women in orange carve their black
on white wanting to be known and not
known facing the known and the unknown

                        Shadows no one wants to see

In the umbra of the jailhouse
Men and women begin to see—and reseed

Not a dramatic   reconstruction   but
a culmination that keeps on
culminating
a process of un-welding   a re-forging

Soldering together metallic
fragments   of an interrupted life   a series of battles
won   and not   one and not
completing the story of an undoing
and in so-doing
construct a re-doing

scars
remain
a body
a map
upon which
blood
was spilled

Some comfort themselves
in the land of *tell no one nothin'*
I ain't no snitch
Not even about oneself

No one ever knows the whole truth
What goes on behind the seens
I caught a case
If only
It wasn't my fault

If only I had
If only I were
If only I could

Perhaps on every headstone
Not *veni vidi vici* but
No truth on which we stand
One not-knowing under no-God
In a landscape carved in mirrors

All Dorothy had
to do
was put on red shoes
Men and women use a pencil
not to be a disappeared
Not a (k)not

Three-inch pencils and paper in hand
(one eraser each)
They (can) become the authors
of their own—cells

Barred from a window
in this time and space capsule
marooned inside their cells   selves
with sharpened enough
pencils they break

Clouds pass across   the landscape of the body
texts falling   like stones
into a sea   of longing

         We're all fa(i)lling

Wanting
to be found

Scared
of getting caught

                    The outside world
                         a hard shell
                            Masks
                         are donned
                           gunman
                           robber
                            rapist
                            killer
                           inside
          the classroom hunting
            for words   soft pulp

Can you hold two realities in your head at one time?
You are who you are   You are who you were

The classroom glares
like a radiation chamber
rectangular
funnels of light ricocheting
off walls of concrete and steel
between
more concrete and steel
the stratosphere
of this county jail

Chalkboard littered
with broken psalms
gang
emblems
stories
turn
the classroom into a lighthouse
show
how a pencil can be used
as a laser beam
to illuminate the scars
of those thrashing
about in the waters

Incarceration is being
caught in shark teeth
three rows pointing inward
no time off
for time served
no possibility of parole
another tooth pulling
each one of the men and women
closer to the throat
closer to being swallowed up
Our society's disappeared

We say light is life and dark is death
But when a seed rises above the ground
It starts to die when a baby leaves the womb
It starts to die when the leaves of a tree
Get too much light they wrinkle and fall

What if the shadow is really the light
And the light the shadow

Men and women hidden in the shadows
Because
Tall, black, and short on green
writes the man with the moniker Hallmark
Because
Moms didn't love me writes Shanice
Because
My stepfather said choose me or him
and she chose him writes Janice
I've been homeless since I was twelve
When I refused to do the laundry she burned my books writes Peter
That way I learned the importance of education
My babysitter made me stick
my pee-pee in my sister writes Tom

Because
Because
Because

How many crimes
are committed
in the name of
I exist I matter

How many crimes
in the name of
I exist I matter
And you're going to pay

Let us set up a memorial

DEDICATED TO ALL
MEN AND WOMEN LIVING INSIDE

Let's announce in the obituaries
The names of those
Who serve on the battlefield
of society's wastelands

The sores and wounds
of outrageous fortune
Living in a sea amongst us
Seen and not seen
Sewn and not sewn
in the seams of prison walls

Who will catch me if I fall
asks the young man with a swollen eye
Jermaine
We're all looking for a father
protector
Some call this God
Some call this a black hole
Step right up   take your pick

Father is
Just like those corny greeting cards
Joe with the broken teeth writes
Father is
Love
Protection
Who to call at night when
lights
go
out

Who to ask when *what should I do*
escapes between lips under a no-moonlit ceiling
buzzing with strips of white light

Net under the tightrope
Web under the feet
White root arcing up through the soil
On which s/he stands

One nation
Under God

Wanting to be known
and not known
facing God
facing Father

*We are all
perpetrators we are all
victims* Lee circle-writes
he watched his father
beat up his mother
who said *you are
just like your father*
and *I became
my father* in jail
for domestic ferocity

Steve watched
his mother
pickpocket his father
He became
his mother
and *stole only so much*
that the victim
would notice
him as little
as his mother did

Is it okay if I walk around asks Apelu
thin in his twenties
long braid down his back
hands
knees
neck
eyes constantly fidgeting
My leg hurts
it's where I got shot

He limps along into his release
Unable to run
catch the bus
as it sped past his stop
last time he was out

I can't catch up to all I missed out on
an ink tear at the corner of his eye

I saw a girl on the bus wearing a tee-shirt that said
I spent time in Alcatraz

Mister refuses
to allow anyone
to call him
by his first name

I won't cry
I promised myself
I wouldn't cry

He cries as he reads
about being tied
to a beam
in the basement
of his father's
home beaten senseless
a beam   an extension cord
crying and reading

Smack
The classroom door slams
open   ghostly pale   sharp-jawed
a deputy barks
the call back
to the six dorms
on the lower level
of one of seven buildings
of this one county jail

Six warehouses
cast in the gray fog
of perspiration and boredom
Toilets unstalled

side by side
along a wall mirrored
by single cots rowed
inches apart divided by
long steel picnic tables
nailed to the floor
Except *it ain't no picnic*

Six dorms
designed for forty-five men
now holding sixty
soon to be seventy
or eighty set beneath
seven administrative offices
hovering above four rounded windows
to keep two   four   six
eyes on two-hundred-and-forty
men day and night   week by week
month by month   year by year
One man worth
thirty dollars a day

Count!
the deputy a master
in the playground
he wishes he had been
always in his grasp
a pen a pad of paper
no more rustling
of writings   whispers
to neighbors finger tapping

A Dorm, Adam, stand up!
Three men
shoot to their feet

Checked off
with a black ballpoint pen
black a color forbidden
to *inmates* except for skin
A number scribbled on a pad
clipped to a brown board

B Dorm, Baker!

There's no one from B Dorm in here
offers a man
face tattooed   abandoned at five
ping-ponged between meth-relatives
He ran away at twelve
with a dog   a girl   a lifetime of prison
His face tattooed
so no one will mess with me

The officer glares
in caricature *What about*
be quiet don't you understand?

E Dorm, Edward!
Five men
shuffle to their feet
Centuries masked
behind bowed heads   silent lips
Yes massa

F, Frank Dorm!
The last
stands to be counted
The one beaten with
an extension cord tied
to a beam in a basement

Men in orange
stand to be counted
Clock on the wall
ticking above mounted
One two buckle your shoe
Three four knock at the door
Deputy soon to Iraq
will be called black body bags
back home will be hauled
No more standing
to be counted
Clock ticking
on the wall mounted

Three hots and a cot
The three R's
Revive
Resuscitate
Relieve

People come to jail hungry
says Bobby
*It's horrible to see how hungry
people get   all they do is take
drugs they don't eat
they don't have money*

Three hots and a cot
The three R's
              Revive
              Resuscitate
              Relieved
Not to be on the streets

Men and women in orange grow like trees
Where there is no light or air
When they come back from wind and sun
       Stumps   emaciated

This is an escape says Leo side-eyed
second night
after a month on the street
cheekbones jutting in his gaunt face
*When I'm out there hustling it's hard
Jail is a chance to come back to ground*

A man whose name was heard
as *De Juan* Of John until written down *Da Juan*
his mother hoped he would be The One
Released this morning
Tall with long dreadlocks gap-toothed smile
crying out his poem about his girlfriend
having an abortion without telling him

George has a dream that Da Juan is up on the roof
calling down *Help me*   The men laugh
their way   of saying
what can not be put   into words

Verwana small compact
looks five months pregnant and doesn't know if she is
I don't know if I can see a doctor for that in jail

From an infection *I been deaf in one ear since I was 5*
her speech thick She could
have had surgery
my mamma didn't want me to

She doesn't tell anyone she can't hear
I don't want them to treat me different

Given a communication device at court
to hear the case against her
I realized that maybe some of the things
that are wrong are because I can't hear
I didn't want to take them off!

Jail is mommy
prison is big daddy
writes the pumped-muscled
tattooed-from-head-to-foot
leader-of-the-gang
caller-of-the-shots

— I carried the drugs for him
writes Anisha tossing back her braids—

He tried to throw me off the roof
Tameika whose piece on how many times she's been inside
(64 at the age of 25)
gets published clandestinely in a magazine
Last week bald head glowing through Mission Street smoky
night air shaking in her joneses   the barest of cotton shrouds
Remember your story you got published? Crouching
close calling through her gray haze *Tameika Tameika Tameika*

Tameika
Short plump   as much snap
crackle and pop
as Rice Krispies
Her breakfast and supper
(free school lunches)

The first day
second day
the third day
fourth day
she sat at the back
chest out
arms folded booming
I don't want to be here!
I want to be taken out of this class!

Her name for the instructor
Leave it to Beaver
Cornball
Don't disrespect me was her comeback
when urged to write something
 anything
You're only doing that because I'm black

Instructor's comeback
Don't disrespect me
You're only doing that
because I'm white

The women laughed
high-fived
Tameika too

Tameika stood on her head
Gyrating   eyes ahead
Stood by the board   licking her lips
Shook her hips   breasts   head
Sometimes tried to get the instructor
to dance   with her

        Day four of week four
    She wrote about being raped and beaten
    by an ex-partner *when ever he sees me*
    I deserve it because I broke his heart

    He tried to throw her off a roof
        He's still my man

Jinelle says
You should follow me around one day
see what my day is like
She refuses to write any thing any time
She refuses to crack the code
to keep *me and mine* safe

She doodles an egg nestling in straw
six months pregnant with one seeing eye
the other shot the same day the father of her child
gushed a river of bullet blood

And then Timothy S
who writes about looking after his disabled father
who describes how he loved school
But that ain't cool in my neighborhood
So he blew it off to fit in
with boys he called kin

A week after back to the streets
shot twice in the chest
dumped
from a car on Potrero and 17th

Some blame his old violence
Some blame the woman he was seeing
Bad news they mutter shaking their heads
Some blame his death on a relapse

What kind of life is it
When a 25 year old man is shot twice
in the chest and dumped on the street
The only way to deal with the pain
Have someone to blame

Pain ekes out
Word by stone
Stone by word
On a dead man's grave

Whatever is alive keeps growing
The man is dead
So the story grows
Until it too is forgotten

The man is dead
And so the story grows
Until he too is forgotten
A monument
To the tune of the unknown
African American

steel bunks
steel toilets
uniforms—black and orange
judges
lawyers— defense and offense
turn
away from their shadows instead shadow puppets
dance to the glaring light of the courtroom
stocked with thick books
paper white
plastered over black bodies
the black   the brown
where white fears to tread

If you're white you done something real wrong—Terrance

                                      black   brown
                  black black
            brown brown
                        black black
                black black
               white black
             brown brown
     brown black   black
     black   black brown
           brown white
           brown black
     brown   brown black
         black black black
        jail probation prison
           parole prison
           prison prison
   parole jail   probation prison

I caught a case

                                          happenstance

                Lalo is four-foot-something
                  swam across the border
            from a river town in Nicaragua
       An endless current erupts from his mouth
                  None of it makes sense
             like listened to him no one has

Suddenly he drops
out of class   accused by fellow rapists murderers thieves
of plagiarizing a life story from a textbook

O what a tangled web we weave

              Lalo can't stanch the flow from his mouth
            A veteran a Sandinista O what tales he could tell
              less hazardous to steal a life from where else

Marco ex-Marine tall wily
born in southern climes
High cheekbones stiff upright
one of the youngest of fourteen
kicked to the curb
bristles when others play around
as if
life is some kind of war game
                              and it is

Monday Marco
drops out of the reserves
turns poems on the wheel of his addiction
and the crumbs of his shame-love
for a woman who used to be a man
who waits for him on the outside
and reads his poetry at the public library
where others gather to call forth
the luminescence of loved ones
through the crack of indifference

Tony swells like a balloon—jail food carbs no exercise
As the jailhouse scribe
trades love
letters to girlfriends and wives
for commissary snacks
ramen noodles   tears roll down stubbly cheeks
as he calculates
in black on white losses and gains
how much he misses his seven year old daughter

Friday Tony gets out
He runs into a woman on 7th Street
By the courthouse off they go to get high
Gets arrested a week later
Back recalibrating his story in two with more

Hey Alberto what's your dorm
You said your AJ whispers orange
jailhouse espadrilles slapping on concrete

No one should never call anything yours
cause when you get out you have nothing

Never call anything yours then
nothing can be taken

Wednesday night chatting outside a downtown
bistro full on crepes   pommes frites   du vin
street curtained by blue tarp
                         Shhh
                         emerges voice irate
                         We're trying to sleep

Never call anything yours
then nothing can be taken from you
Not even peace and quiet

Tuesday night
Two men shot dead
One twenty-three one fifty-one
Ollis calls   twenty-eight   two years out of jail
I woke up at 5am I saw the news on TV
I wrote a poem can I read it to you
It's called Coulda been me

His spilling of words ends with
the blood spilled from my body
I looked towards the skies
Then the breath left my lungs
And I closed my eyes
Still cogitating in silence
I observed the death of the two brothers
Feeling the pain of their loved ones
Hearing the cries of their mothers
So before I began to write about my feelings
I turned off the TV
And the first thing I thought was
Damn that coulda been me

Wednesday night
Antonio joins the class
No more than twenty
face pimpled eyes soft
The first assignment is to write
your life story in twenty minutes

I didn't know
it was going to be like this
I thought it was going to be quiet
His chin droops to his chest
My brother was shot dead last night
They shot him four or five times
Antonio's eyes an ocean
The water rises
My brother was only 23

Leo gap-toothed grin
encircled in thick steel
cabled to the wall
not allowed belts ties or elastic
abandoned wire could do worse

This keeps me safe Leo jokes
On his arm a tattoo 5150 lock-up for mental illness
Both parents drug addicts
one kidnapped and abused him and his sister
Nabbed by the FBI kids
fostered mother overdosed
I don't know where my dad is

Who says only mothers
sacrifice for their children
Don't children sacrifice
for their mothers

Cowboy McGee wears his mother's depression
Harold his mother's crack habit
Phelicia her mother's rage
Swimming sinking in the same river of grief

Two Morris brothers ten months apart
Your poor mother someone says
What about us they retort

They roll out the corny clichéd
drumbeat that echoes through walls
Babies having babies
As if

Two heads taller than most
Jiménez is back loping
into the windowless classroom
a week month year or two in between
                        streets

                                        Black-framed
                                        jail glasses

wall guarded eyes
an old scar cuts through
an eyebrow
eyelid skewed

Fifty
cropped hair clipped beard
orange pants shirt hang loosely lace-less orange sneakers
arms long and ropey hands oversized rough
overbite jaw wired shut after the *incident*
one lifetime on the streets

What lies inside the heart
of a man with six children abandoned
How do hands that write so gently
                Inject a needle
                Punch a child
                Shoot a man
                Break into houses
Steal from sisters brothers aunts uncles?

What is the purpose of a life of a man
who has spent most of his fifty years
in the ashes of pipe dreams?

Jiménez strung out on methadone
In exchange for three hots and a cot
And not having to prowl tarred streets
Stealing robbing cheating

Jiménez copies the words
Buddhists say this is it
Our lives are not a deviation
Pins them to his cell wall

Then he says *I want to think about it*
Then he gets transferred

    jail   court jail court jail

              prison

                          parole jail
                              court jail court jail prison

            parole   jail

                      court   jail   prison

                                            parole

    jail   court jail court jailjailjail prison

Rogelio Monday
forty-six birthdays uncelebrated
adopted by abusers   drugs *I found*
people who accepted me wife
in downtown jail *relapse* both
working to get their son back from CPS
I don't want him to suffer
what I did I don't want   to repeat the cycle

Jaquan
two months paroled away
from his neighborhood   violated
How could I stay
away from my friends and family
                they all live
there that's where I belong
                I have nowhere else

Steve
gray
strands woven into
dreadlocks
his story of trying
to grow
in the south *sitting at the back*
                of the bus he escaped
California and drugs
How would your life
have been if drugs were legal?
He can not stop laughing   Big belly laugh

Chuy's flat got raided   a gang sweep
I never go out to keep out of trouble
white powder was found   locked up downtown
waiting for analysis
My parole officer said they already knew it was flour
He is kept inside for a week
Thirty dollars a day another man/woman down

Harold in a spat with his wife
She called the police and said I was beating her even
my lawyer didn't believe it his cheating
made her give another body to the prison industry
That's two happy now

It's my time to call 911
Kalann the only one who talks
about being beaten by a woman

Wednesday night a man
with the same surname as Elvis
sang
a love song   In the men's eyes
                    naked pain

Matthew discarded
on the street at four
group home
                foster home group
    home foster
                home group

Eeny meeny miny mo
catch this tiger by the toe—except he uses the n word
Look at my house he points to a cell
Bedded behind plexiglass in a double bunk
—one muscle-y man atop another
arms spread they touch both walls—
Matthew is home in jail concrete
city pavement the other

Gary aka Terminator
tattooed teardrop marking him killer
eyes mirror (plexi)glass and steel

*Can you please stop talking so
the others can write* The room
stills men crouch duck and cover

Terminator bares his teeth
Do you know who I am looming close pumping
muscle beneath hard fat jail food

Do you know who I am
a right thing at the right time
He now helps to hand out pencils
and paper   face soft yielding
Can I help you Miss another child-man looking
for a place a body to call home

Jason swirls
the revolving door a dance of dervishes
I knew what I was doing divorced lost
his kids a two week stealing spree

wanting
to get caught just like Pinguino
who threw a brick and sat
stooped   waiting for the police

Deshawn writes about the slave master
the whip passed through generations
landing in his father's hands
how he was *baptized in someone else's rage*

*I am like my father I am
not like my father* Dwight's left
when he was eleven turned up left again
when he was thirty-five

I feel like I was abandoned all over again
Tears streaming down his scar-gashed face
I love my father but not that father

Father was
Hells Angel so is son father
took drugs so does son father
beat women so does son
father a disappeared in Hawaii
son a disappeared in jail

RM twenty-six got out of Pelican Bay State Prison
The worst of the worst of the worst warehouse
Rode the bus twelve hours back
to a house lived in by his *play sister*
Only out for seven days last
time never reported to parole—three months this
I am one of the lucky ones I have a father
He took me to the streets taught me how to sell heroin
So join my life in Misery the name of my poem
Twenty-six and counting down

Manolo starts *Hello family*
Hello comes the echo
through steel bars a hearth

Hello it's me
Adam
opera singer—rent boy
to fill a crack habit—
I'm as queer as a square grape
The others laugh some
might be homophobic on the outs
in here it is all up for grabs

Gordo lives on the street
when not in the Big House
Never call your cell your home
being the place broken
into like so many broken
bottles collected holding broken
dreams to erect a somebody
I started to feel good about myself when I became
homeless I found people who were just like me

Why does no one talk about the happy
times in the camps asks a holocaust survivor
Why does no one talk about the happy
times in jail asks Eddy calls his cell *home*

Tim arranges   his lanky body
on a bench nailed   to the floor   long fingers splayed
outward legs   akimbo
I have nobody and nothing out there
Now I can be content

Jail is mommy prison is big daddy
grins the pumped-muscled
tattooed-from-head-to-foot
leader-of-the-gang caller-of-the-shots

Buck-toothed Jason with the sly smile
Panic. Pain-C?

Charlie Seneca gets out   shoots up   dies
resurrected after   nine months   in jail
            the drugs are too strong

Sean Reynolds at a reading in October on the outs
smart suit   button-down pink shirt
smooth shaven
                   kills himself in November

DeMario Atkins
run over by a bus or car or plane
escaping the po po

He died so the rest of us could live
The bible quoted   Jesus Christ
Religious predators leave scriptures chalked
on the blackboard the only Ones
not denied entry into the underworld

Why couldn't he live so the rest of them can?

Jaquan Davis
Sonia Brown
Jamal Atkins
DeMario Atkins
Rosa Ramirez
Charlie Seneca
Shanika White
Christopher Johnson
Timothy Scott
Sean Reynolds
No battle hymn of the republic here
Amen

If you are not called
by your name who are you

Rodney is Chivo or Shark
Juan is Shorty
Mister won't let anyone call him
by any name front or back
Deondrick is Li'l B
Federico is AJ or Charlie
Hernan is Chino or Blow

Their only ID a jail card or *A Grain Of Sand*
On Which My Life Story Is Written
                                      by Joshua aka Toast

How many crimes are written
in the name *I exist I matter*

How many in the name *I do not
and you are going to pay*

Two men read aloud war stories
One from El Salvador
One Hunters Point

The men believe the world is divided
Predators and prey
If you are not you are

If only we could see
ourselves as we are shadow light

When I'm out there   Temo mid March
mid sentence
I can't keep still
           running here
     running there
Thin railed he
          jumps to the
     side and back again
hands in the air sculpting a
pillar
                    drugs
help me stay center

What would happen if
Temo stopped   stood still

What would happen if
we all   stood still

Incarceration
Incanceration
change of one letter
change of one cell

        Jailhouse saying
what doesn't kill you
makes you stronger
              drug addiction
                      the revolving door
                              makes them weaker

Incarceration
caught in shark teeth
three rows pointing inward
One falls out a lawyer fucks up
A judge sleeps on the job

Society's cancer
No time off for time served
No possibility of parole

Another tooth pulling
closer to the throat closer
to being swallowed

Men and women have to be
their own vigilante

Department of Corrections   *as if*
the ills   of poverty   degradation
can be corrected   by incarceration

Reggie
eyeglass arm
gray duct-taped *ghetto*
style grins
lips parted
flecks of spit
at the corners
three months gone
another
four to serve

I was riding no back light
on my bike I was on parole got
seven months   a mistake
shark teeth

Imagine a glass timer
The bottom full of sand
Turn it upside down
What would life be like

I'd take my son to the beach every day

I'd get married to my girlfriend who died last year

I'd choose my homie

I'da stayed in school

I wouldn't let my girl have an abortion

I wouldn't take the first hit of crack

Can you fucking   believe   it   Erik
swollen   red rage   *I loaded
up the van*   *with the cameras TVs
jewelry I just peeled*   *I told my friend
move the van round*   *the back he drove off*
         what a bastard

You should hate me   he writes
I'm the fuck-up   *who snorted
your jewelry*   *computers*   *and DVD players*

December   *caught a case*
in a stolen car
protests   *I paid for half of it*

January February March April
Erik hands over story after story
It's my life   *I want it published*
In May   ashen-faced asks
What if   *one of us stole your car
and my writing was in it
that wouldn't be right would it*

silhouette and sunlight caught

Sharon sits with her hands   over her face
so she can sleep   behind bars
of her own   making
she puts strips of colored tape
across and down her face   like an African warrior
runs around the classroom   chanting
                                    awake

Aisha writes
I don't feel fear
I didn't feel anything
when I was raped

Morning sick given a pregnancy test
even though *I can't be pregnant I'm gay*
then she figures she was raped
when passed out on a sidewalk
At least I knew who raped me the other time

In her thirties
in and out of jail
since 18   or 13   or 15
It all became the same
at some point
The war on drugs

I'm institutionalized
I want to be out
but when I get out of jail
she puts her hands up to her face
I don't know what to do
I don't know where to go

When I'm out I don't know
how to do anything
everything is rushing at me
all at once

The son of Gregory Johnson murdered
one year ago fifteen minutes a month
with a jailhouse psychiatrist
One of the lucky ones she says

Let us set up a memorial
**DEDICATED
TO ALL THE MEN AND WOMEN
DEAD INSIDE**
caught in the current
back back
back back back
backedy backedy back

Hunters Point
their neighborhood they call HP
underserved   underappreciated   underfed

Up on the hill on the other side
of town
over
served
over
appreciated
over
fed
Pacific Heights no one calls PH

No PH
only wounds that show   and those that do not

In a corridor
a metal coop six feet high
outside gray filing cabineted admin offices
a sign hangs on one of the bars
Don't talk to inmates in cages

A man with the name of an angel drifts
into class after a gone year
skin bones methamphetamine
it lets me have sex and sex and sex
survivor or not of repeated rape remnants
of city fog lingering in bleary eyes
another on a parole violation—
one plus one plus ten plus twenty plus
rapidly rising rithmetic of the prison industry

How you doin
he mumbles stuttering like before
weeks spider letters scribble   images seeking web
Thursday night before   unlocked
or not back   to the streets
sex slaves Lucifer   his pencil breathes
The others in silence   hands laced like prayer
until The End   *That was a bad acid trip*
Angel man raises eyes fog cleared

Malek
Is that why your speech is messed up?
Before no one had called attention to angel man struggling sounds
no one with   no problem   breaking
into houses   cars   aiming guns   at heads   pulling triggers

The head of the man with the name
of an angel
whips
down *No* and he scribbles
more
The others read their horror
stories until class reaches
The End   Angel man waves thin
spider fingers
It's short he insists
through corridor footsteps echoing louder
When I was five my father sodomized me
He pushed my head into the couch
and fucked me up the ass
He kept on doing it for years
When he didn't shove my head
into the couch he used a cushion
or a pillow   That's why I stutter

What if the body is real and the mind isn't
If 'tis nobler in the mind to suffer the slings and arrows
than the body drown in a sea of misfortune

Another man   same class   different day   different name
survivor or not of different family   The End
Scapegoat is the sins of the people projected onto a goat
that is tied up and burned at the stake That be me
                            A smile or not flickers across his face

When I've been down so long
it looks like up to me
Dominique   eyes
the color of a moss-coated ocean

I'm big black and short on green
writes the tall dark handsome man
This is the last time   more than seventeen years
revolving door *this time* after eighteen months splits
with a swish and a nod

Three weeks later a hospital emergency room
one foot amputated diabetes
now back on crutches with a plastic leg
flesh colored—but not his flesh
son of a father who left   came back to take
son to the movies to a theme park give a gift bicycle
or said he was and *didn't didn't didn't*
the son of a mother's guilt and frustration
making him the center of the universe
until she met another man with other children
the new family a melting pot where everyone got burned
no more center he does not see the irony
of the women he pimped as crutches
now 45 going on 96 tries
to solder where he was at 10

His left foot gone
he hides why he is in   *this time*
as he hobbles around with a prosthesis that hurts
the nub of a leg whole and no longer
just like when a little boy
whole   no longer
un-*centered*   without a foot
that once anchored him   as his mother had
even when she took   away the ground

When told *As an adult no one is that special*
to be at the center of the universe
he writes *What do they know small white full on green*

*Do prisoners
make prison
work
because they feel they deserve it?*
asks Tony
I'm used to it
he says
*Just using the skills
I learned when I was adopted*

Little children flushed with hope
devolved into adults barred

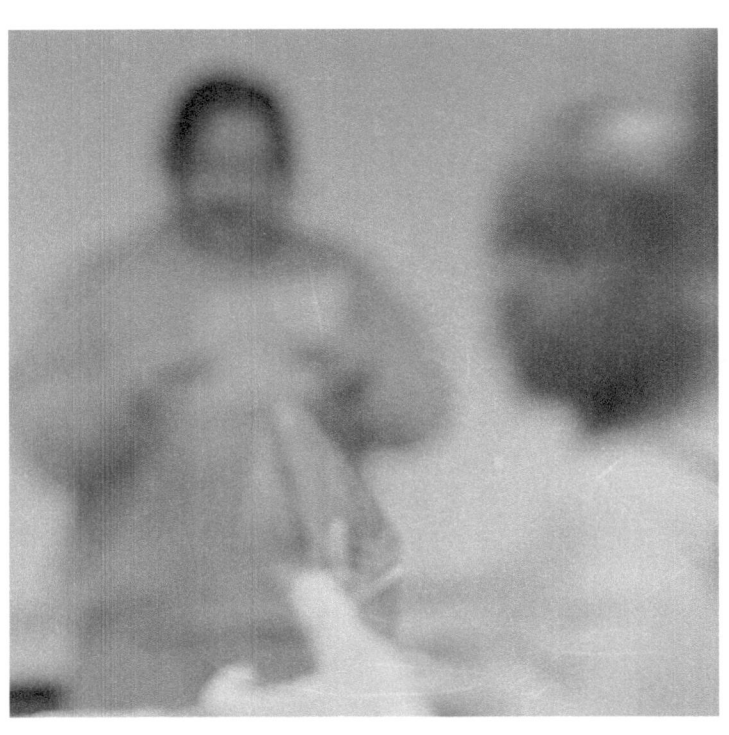

air vents clumped with orange lint
George unwarned moved downtown

uniform(s) orange and black
Fallo due to be released sent on a warrant to Arizona

Count!
Donnie untold incarcerated an extra month

intercoms buzz
Randy (white) furloughed five days for his daughter's wedding

men scream
David (black) unfurloughed for his grandma's funeral

4:30 am wake up call
Dorm E lockdown five days no visitors

cell built for one   double bunk for two
lie upon lie

Ronnie *I am the loneliest lonely*

Say Happy Birthday Marquand
blurts in the gray hallway
laughing shyly head down

Did you do anything to celebrate?
Lips curl *Like what? Stand in a garbage can?*

Happy Birthday Tesfay
turns 19 clad in orange
from war torn Eritrea
to war torn Oakland
His family visits every weekend
His mother's lips worrying away
Why did we move
all the way here to another war

At the mouth of the delta into which lost dreams disappear
Nik runs to the front of class glasses off-kilter
face mottled bloated   Hulking men
trying to fill themselves on child-sized meals
miniature cartons of orange juice and milk packets of
crackers so small even airlines do not use them

I've just written a series
Nik pants   *Writing out the Pain*
Tears roll
down
his acned face   as he reads
abuse   by babysitter   family friend
another family friend   father   mother
his abuse of wife daughter family friend

Alvin
When I come to class
I feel a space
I make my peace
I know I'm lying

Chaz
My mother tried to abort me
She sent me to foster care when I was nine
I want to win the National Book Award to show her
I'm worth something

Why don't you ever write about the happy times
says Leonardo
Fuck off answers Brian

Antony says
We're like pussycats in this class
You should see what we do to each other
in the dorms   last night after class
one OG whipped another one with a chair.

Michael does not know who his father is
His mother was a crack addict

I forgave her when she went into recovery
I don't take drugs He sells them

He is angry at his cousin
How could he sell drugs to my mother?

He sells drugs to other people's mothers
I know what I'm doing but I don't care

To care you have to love yourself
                                and I don't

Jail is a vacation
writes Joseph *a rest*
from bills   relationships   family

The street is more dangerous than jail Arelus
The street has no deputies to control anyone

He is seen from a streetcar window
a cracked man in a crack haze
zigzagging from one side of the street to the other
back and again and back chuckle-talking to himself

60 men sleep
eat
urinate
defecate
masturbate
shower
shave
cut hair
work out
write letters
write poems
write songs
make collect calls
beg for favors
beg for quiet
beg to be left alone
pray
play cards
gamble with commissary
read
borrow
steal
watch TV
in 1 room
That'll be the all of it

1 deputy
bored
on full alert
in less than 60

you can not tell the story of jail
without telling the story of the prisoner
you can not tell the story of the prisoner
without telling the story of the prison industry

the truth
the whole truth
nothing but the truth
so help us

I'll be here for a minute
means a month   a year   a decade
till death do us part

A turkey vulture lumbers skyward
and plops down on the highest limb
of a tall gray pine

Another flies up   lands

And another

another

How can that limb carry the weight
of so many lumbering birds

How do birds that carry so much weight fly?

In the beginning there was the Word
And the word was with God
And the word was God

In the beginning there was the Word
And the word was with Us
And the word was
R-E-S-P-E-C-T The word was L-O-V-E

Guards
afraid
of their shadows   lie in wait
a scolding here   a lockup there
What is it about stand straight
you don't understand?
guards knowing
their shadows   bring in an illicit
hamburger here/a book there

If not for the grace of God

A guard tells me eyes still bright
I only have fourteen years left

Another guard   another place   another time
Sallow beneath fluorescent lights
Takes off his wedding ring when
he gets to work
I never let anyone know I'm married

Another guard
If you don't like it here don't come
another shows off his travel pictures
another gets caught selling drugs
another is transferred from *being too physical*
another says *I got into trouble when I was young*
This is the only job I could get

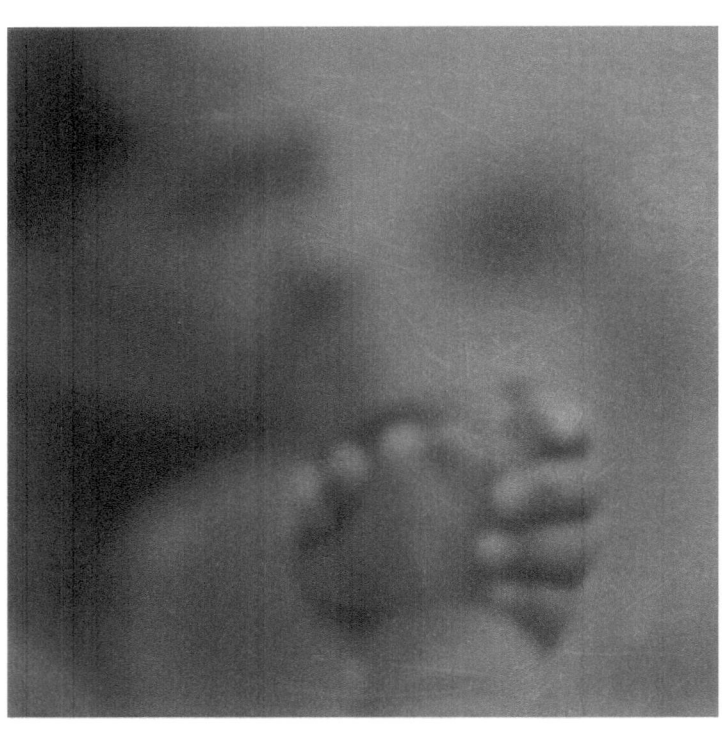

A CO with the big
belly-oh
sucking on
an ice cream stick
You could
be investigated
he says   seeing instructor
talk to a student after class

His belly-oh heavy with hate
disgust roiling in his
gut
     stomach
          swollen
               fury
                    spite

How could he be light?
Oh
    if one might
tell you kind sir
stop it with the slur
One does not need an investigator
to find out what your problem is
it's writ large all over you Sarge

A public celebration outside the jail
A picture of Yoko and John hangs above a banner
Imagine
Give peace a chance

Speaker after speaker
Celebrity after celebrity
District Attorney Sheriff Mayor
celebrating their funding of programs that
lead to an end to violence and reduction of crime

outside walls
behind which is committed
The Greatest Crime of All

Though I am physically locked behind these walls
I take a moment now and then to sneak away,
unnoticed, and undetected
They think that I am here, number 2085814 accounted for
but I have fooled them once again
for I am not here at all
This most ancient form of magic once again
transports me to far away lands
where I can dance with the trees
and sleep by the moon
Though they claim to see me   I won't be back soon
You see I'm writing through walls   this I can do
There's no law against it   for me   or for you

Gregory Johnson's son murdered a year ago
Grief so thick he can't talk about it until now
through his engravings black on white

crimes solved and not

a bar town but not that kind of bar

Staring at life's distortions through plexiglass

MARGO PERIN is the author of *The Opposite of Hollywood* and the contributing editor of *Only the Dead Can Kill: Stories from Jail* and *How I Learned to Cook & Other Writings on Complex Mother Daughter Relationships.* She is the poet of San Francisco's public memorial *Spiral of Gratitude* (collaboration with artist Shimon Attie/BALEAF) and the Sonoma Area Coordinator for California Poets in the Schools.

A nominee for the Pushcart Prize, Margo Perin has been featured by *BBC News, BBC World Service Outlook, O, The Oprah Magazine,* Heyday/PEN's *Fightin' Words, The Press Democrat, The San Francisco Chronicle,* Mexico's *El Petit Journal,* Holland's *Psychologie* and on TV and radio. She has received awards from the Creative Work Fund, the California Arts Council, San Francisco Arts Commission, Creative Sonoma, and Poets & Writers. Among other teaching artist residencies, Margo facilitates healing through poetry and creative writing workshops, including for children and adults dealing with trauma, incarcerated and targeted youth and adults, medical professionals, and people with cancer and other life-threatening illnesses.

www.margoperin.com

www.ingramcontent.com/pod-product-compliance
Lightning Source LLC
Chambersburg PA
CBHW021955290426
44108CB00012B/1074